INTER A CESSION
WITH GOD

An Intercessory Prayer Guide

Sherita Mitchell

Published by Spines
ISBN: 979-8-89569-161-8

Contents

Dedication

With tears in my eyes and a brief pause due to overwhelming gratitude, I honor my mentor and spiritual mother, the powerfully anointed teacher and intercessor—the late Dr. Sheraine Lathon. Her ministry was a beacon of wisdom, compassion, and spiritual insight that profoundly shaped my understanding of prayer. Dr. Lathon's guidance went beyond mere instruction; she modeled what it meant to live a life fully devoted to God, demonstrating the power of fervent, faith-filled intercession. She taught me that prayer is not just about speaking words but about listening, waiting, and aligning oneself with the will of God.

Alongside her, the late Dr. Clifford E. Turner also played a significant role in my development as an intercessor. Dr. Turner was a spiritual giant whose teachings and prophetic insight challenged me to go deeper in my walk with God. His emphasis on spiritual discipline and his unwavering commitment to the Word of God inspired me to cultivate a life of consistent prayer and intercession. Together, Dr. Lathon and Dr. Turner were a dynamic duo who were instrumental in my spiritual growth and teaching. They nurtured my calling, helping me to understand the depth and breadth of intercessory prayer.

Even though they are no longer with us, their legacies continue to live on in the lives of those they impacted. I dedicate this book to them in their honor, acknowledging the profound influence they had on my journey. This dedication is more than a tribute; it is a testament to the enduring impact of their ministry and the invaluable lessons they imparted to me. Their teachings have become the foundation upon which my own ministry is built, and I am forever grateful for their wisdom, love, and guidance.

Preface

This book is a guide to provide guidance and help to those who believe they are to be intercessors. I will unlock some hidden truths about prayer and how we pray. This book will help you understand the difference between spiritual warfare, interceding on behalf of yourself and others, and communing with God, as HE commands us to do. I will show you that there is a significant difference between talking or communing with the Father and commanding enemy spirits. Being an intercessor is a great responsibility given by God to His people. I will show you what God is looking for in His intercessors and what qualifies you to stand in the gap for others. I will teach you the importance of living a clean, exemplary life that God deems acceptable by HIM. The Word tells us that God does not hear sinners. You can be a child of God and sin, which could make you a sinner saved by grace.

Knowledge is power, and understanding is worthy to seek after. Strive for understanding of the Word of God. People perish for lack of knowledge. As we embark on the journey of intercessory prayer, my hope is that you gain the necessary tools that will strengthen you in your calling and make you most effective. The prayer of the righteous avails much. The key word here is "righteous."

BEFORE WE START

In a world filled with chaos, uncertainty, and challenges, there is a profound call to return to the basics of our faith. It begins with a humbling of ourselves before the Almighty God, acknowledging our dependence on Him for every breath we take.

2 Chronicles 7:14 (KJV):

"If my people, which are called by my name, shall humble themselves, and pray, and seek my face, and turn from their wicked ways; then will I hear from heaven, and will forgive their sin, and will heal their land."

This verse serves as a foundational truth for every believer. It is a divine invitation and a powerful promise from God. He calls us to humble ourselves, to come to Him in sincere prayer, to seek His presence earnestly, and to turn away from everything that separates us from Him.

When we, as God's people, respond to this call with genuine repentance and wholehearted devotion, we unlock the doors to divine forgiveness and healing. The power of intercessory prayer lies in this very principle—our willingness to stand in the gap for others, to plead for mercy, and to seek God's intervention.

Before we dive into the heart of what it means to be an intercessor, let us first reflect on this powerful promise. Let it resonate in your spirit and ignite a passion within you to be a person who seeks God's face, who stands in the gap, and who helps usher in His healing and restoration.

As we embark on this journey together, may we remember that the path to effective intercession starts with humility, prayer, and a heart turned fully toward God. Let us prepare ourselves to stand in the gap with clean hands, pure hearts, and a resolute spirit, knowing that our God is faithful to hear, forgive, and heal.

Chapter 1

Let's Enter A Session With God

Inter A Cession or INTERCESSION

So many things I have learned under their tutelage and the guidance of the Holy Spirit by divine revelation. With all of that said, let us dive right in. Let us first define what an intercessor is.

INTERCESSOR MEANING & REFERENCES FROM THE BIBLE

One that will Pray on Behalf of Other People, Places, and Situations.

1. **Ephesians 6:12 (KJV):**"For we wrestle not against flesh and blood, but against principalities, against powers, against the rulers of the darkness of this world, against spiritual wickedness in high places." This verse emphasizes that our struggles are not merely against physical or earthly challenges but against spiritual forces of evil.

One Who Will Stand in the Gap for you in Prayer.

Intercessory prayer, or praying on behalf of others, is a concept that appears throughout the Bible. While the term "intercessory" itself not mentioned in translations, the act of intercession is frequently depicted. Here are some key scriptures that highlight intercessory prayer:

Genesis 18:22-33: Abraham intercedes for Sodom and Gomorrah, pleading with God to spare the city if he found one righteous person there.

1. **Exodus 32:11-14**: Moses intercedes on behalf of the Israelites after they sinned by worshipping the golden calf. Moses pleads with God to turn away His wrath and not destroy them.
2. **Numbers 14:13-20**: Moses again intercedes for the Israelites when they rebel against God in the wilderness, asking God to forgive their sin.
3. **1 Samuel 12:23**: Samuel says, "As for me, far be it from me that I should sin against the Lord by ceasing to pray for you; and I will instruct you in the good and the right way." Here, Samuel commits to intercessory prayer for the people of Israel.
4. **Job 42:10**: After Job prays for his friends, who had spoken wrongly about God, God restores Job's fortunes and gives him twice as much as he had before.
5. **Isaiah 53:12**: This prophecy about the Messiah says, "For he bore the sin of many, and made intercession for the transgressors," indicating that Jesus would function as an intercessor.
6. **Romans 8:26-27**: The Apostle Paul writes about the Holy Spirit interceding for believers: "In the same way, the Spirit helps us in our weakness. We do not know what we ought to

pray for, but the Spirit himself intercedes for us through wordless groans."

7. **Hebrews 7:25**: Referring to Jesus, it says, "Therefore he is able to save completely those who come to God through him, because he always lives to intercede for them."

8. **1 Timothy 2:1**: Paul urges believers to make intercessions: "I urge, then, first of all, that petitions, prayers, intercession, and thanksgiving be made for all people."

These passages illustrate that intercessory prayer is a vital part of the biblical tradition, demonstrating the importance of praying on behalf of others, places, and situations.

Prayer Warrior

The term "Prayer Warrior" is not explicitly mentioned in the Bible, but the concept of devotion and devoted to prayer and engaging in spiritual warfare through prayer is certainly present throughout the scriptures. A prayer warrior is known to be committed to praying fervently and persistently, often interceding on behalf of others, and battling against spiritual forces through prayer. Here are some key scriptures that align with the idea of being a prayer warrior:

1. **Ephesians 6:18**: After describing the full armor of God, Paul instructs believers to pray: "And pray in the Spirit on all occasions with all kinds of prayers and requests. With this in mind, be alert and always keep on praying for all the Lord's people." This verse emphasizes the importance of continual prayer as part of spiritual warfare.

2. **2 Corinthians 10:3-5**: Paul talks about the spiritual nature of our battles: "For though we live in the world, we do not wage war as the world does. The weapons we fight with are not the

weapons of the world. On the contrary, they have divine power to demolish strongholds. We demolish arguments and every pretension that sets itself up against the knowledge of God, and we take captive every thought to make it obedient to Christ." This passage suggests that prayer and spiritual discipline are key components in overcoming spiritual challenges.

3. **Colossians 4:12**: Paul commends Epaphras, a member of the Colossian church, for his dedication to prayer: "Epaphras, who is one of you and a servant of Christ Jesus, sends greetings. He is always wrestling in prayer for you, that you may stand firm in all the will of God, mature and fully assured." Epaphras, described as someone who is fervently praying for others, which aligns with the concept of a prayer warrior.

4. **James 5:16**: This verse emphasizes the power of prayer: "Therefore confess your sins to each other and pray for each other so that you may be healed. The prayer of a righteous person is powerful and effective." The idea here is that committed, righteous prayer has great power, which is a core belief of those who consider themselves prayer warriors.

5. **Daniel 10:12-13**: Daniel's persistent prayer and fasting for 21 days resulted in a spiritual breakthrough when an angel finally reached him, explaining that his prayer had been heard from the first day but that there was spiritual opposition. This passage illustrates the idea of spiritual warfare and the power of persistent prayer.

These scriptures, while not using the specific term "Prayer Warrior," clearly convey the importance of prayer as a means of spiritual engagement and emphasize the need for vigilance, persistence, and dedication in prayer. This is the essence of what it means to be a prayer warrior in the Christian faith.

One Who Lives a Clean Life

The Bible emphasizes the importance of living a clean, pure, and righteous life in several passages. These scriptures highlight the significance of moral integrity, holiness, and cleanliness in the eyes of God. Here are some key verses that speak to the concept of living a clean life:

1. Psalm 24:3-4:"Who may ascend the mountain of the Lord? Who may stand in his holy place? The one who has clean hands and a pure heart, who does not trust in an idol or swear by a false god."

This passage underscores the need for both clean hands (actions) and a pure heart (inner thoughts and intentions) to be in the presence of God.

2. James 4:8:"Come near to God and he will come near to you. Wash your hands, you sinners, and purify your hearts, you double-minded."

James calls for both outward and inward cleanliness, urging believers to cleanse their actions and purify their hearts.

3. Matthew 5:8:"Blessed are the pure in heart, for they will see God."

Jesus teaches that those who maintain purity in their hearts will have the privilege of seeing God.

4. 2 Corinthians 7:1:"Therefore, since we have these promises, dear friends, let us purify ourselves from everything that contaminates body and spirit, perfecting holiness out of reverence for God."

Paul encourages believers to strive for holiness by purifying themselves from anything that defiles their body or spirit.

5. 1 Peter 1:15-16:"But just as he who called you is holy, so be holy in all you do; for it is written: 'Be holy, because I am holy.'"

This verse emphasizes the call to holiness in all aspects of life, mirroring the holiness of God.

6. Proverbs 4:23: "Above all else, guard your heart, for everything you do flows from it."

This proverb highlights the importance of maintaining a pure heart, as it influences all of one's actions.

7. Philippians 2:15: "So that you may become blameless and pure, 'children of God without fault in a warped and crooked generation.' Then you will shine among them like stars in the sky."

Paul urges believers to live blameless and pure lives, standing out in a world that is often morally corrupt.

8. 1 John 3:3: "All who have this hope in him purify themselves, just as he is pure."

The expectation of Christ's return motivates believers to live pure lives, reflecting the purity of Christ.

These scriptures collectively emphasize the importance of living a life that is clean, both outwardly and inwardly, to maintain a close relationship with God and reflect His holiness to the world.

INTERCESSION

The word intercession comes from an old Greek word, which was a technical term for one who approaches a king; thus, used to describe prayers approaching God. Our English word intrude comes from this Greek word. Therefore, to intercede is to intrude upon someone on behalf of another. An intercessor is a go-between, someone who pleads the case of another. To intercede is to function as a mediator, much like an attorney who pleads their client's case in a court of law.

An attorney is a person who has learned the laws of the land to represent their clients effectively. There is no such thing as an attorney who does not know the law. Similarly, if you are going to be an intercessor for others, you must know the Word of God thoroughly, just as an attorney knows the law. You need to be able to apply the appropriate scriptures for the person or situation for which you are praying.

- The act of intervening on behalf of others.
- The action of saying a prayer for another person, place, or situation.
- Praying to a deity asking for help for others.

I remember accompanying a friend to court some time ago as her support. When we arrived, we noticed that her attorney was not there. While waiting, the court's bailiff opened the doors and began calling cases on the docket. Since cellular phones are not allowed in the courts, there was no way to reach her attorney's office to find out why they weren't present. My friend started to show signs of anxiety.

As we waited in the back of the courtroom, all the cases were called, but her attorney still hadn't arrived. She asked the judge if she could approach the bench to inform the court that her attorney was a no-show. The judge allowed her to do so and explained that, because her attorney hadn't shown up, her case would have to be rescheduled for about two months later. My friend was visibly upset and disappointed by her attorney's failure to appear.

My friend had hoped her court case would have been resolved that day, but that wasn't the case. I share this story to illustrate a prophetic parallel: As intercessors who go before God on behalf of others, we act much like attorneys who stand before a judge in a court of law. It is of the utmost importance that we show up for people in prayer.

When we neglect our time in prayer as intercessors, we become responsible for delaying someone's breakthrough, especially for those whose faith is still developing and who can't quite manage to pray effectively on their own. People need us to be in our positions of prayer, so they don't end up feeling like my friend did—angry, frustrated, and disappointed with her attorney. Lives can be put on hold when the mediators are not in their rightful place of prayer.

Chapter 2

Do You Qualify To Stand In The Gap Or Be An Intercessor?

In this chapter, we explore the qualities and conditions necessary to be an effective intercessor—someone who stands in the gap on behalf of others in prayer. Being an intercessor is not just about praying for others; it requires a deep commitment to living a life that aligns with God's standards and being someone, whom God can trust to stand in the gap for His people.

1. Ezekiel 22:30: "And I sought for a man among them that should make up the hedge and stand in the gap before me for the land, that I should not destroy it, but I found none."

- This verse highlights God's search for a person who would intercede on behalf of the land to prevent its destruction. It underscores the importance of being available and willing to intercede when God calls, illustrating the profound responsibility and privilege of standing in the gap.

2. Matthew 22:14:"For many are called, but few are chosen."

- This verse reminds us that while many may feel the urge or call to pray for others, only a few are chosen for the specific and serious task of intercession. It suggests that being an intercessor requires more than just the willingness to pray; it requires being chosen by God and living a life that meets His standards.

3. Psalm 24:3-4:"Who may ascend into the hill of the Lord? Or who may stand in His holy place? He who has clean hands and a pure heart, who has not lifted up his soul to an idol, nor sworn deceitfully."

- This passage sets forth the qualifications for those who desire to stand in God's presence. To be an intercessor, one must have clean hands (righteous actions) and a pure heart (righteous motives). This verse emphasizes that moral integrity and purity are essential prerequisites for those who wish to intercede before God.

4. John 9:31:"Now we know that God does not hear sinners; but if anyone is a worshiper of God and does His will, He hears him."

- Here, we see a clear statement about God's responsiveness to those who are righteous and live according to His will. An intercessor must be devoted to God, living a life of obedience, and actively worshiping Him. God listens to those who are aligned with His purposes and are obedient to His commands.

LET'S BREAK THIS DOWN - What is a sinner?

A sinner is a person who commits sins, transgressing against divine laws by engaging in immoral or wrongful acts. In the biblical context, sin is any action, thought, or behavior that goes against God's commands and desires. A sinner is someone who lives a life that is contrary to God's Word and ways, choosing to act in ways that separate them from God.

Sin encompasses not just overt actions, like stealing or lying, but also includes attitudes and thoughts that are inconsistent with God's character, such as pride, envy, and hatred. According to Christian teachings, everyone is born with a sinful nature due to the fall of humanity, but through repentance and faith in Jesus Christ, individuals can be forgiven and restored to a right relationship with God.

Understanding what it means to be a sinner is crucial for recognizing the need for repentance, forgiveness, and a transformed life that aligns with God's will and purpose.

Examples of Types of Sins

- Pride
- Gluttony
- Slothfulness
- Greed
- Idolatry
- Adultery
- Lust
- Rebellion
- Envy
- Killing
- Lying

- Blasphemy against the Holy Spirit (the unpardonable sin)
- Being judgmental
- Selfishness
- Unforgiveness
- Bitterness
- Holding grudges
- Stealing
- Dishonoring your parents

In reference to **Psalm 24:3-4**, which gives us a description of the qualities God looks for in those wanting to connect with Him through intercession, let us explore those four qualifications.

CLEAN HANDS

Having clean hands refers to living a righteous life and performing righteous deeds, while refraining from evil actions. It involves doing what is right and maintaining integrity and good character. The Bible teaches that the blood of Christ cleanses us, providing clean hands that qualify us to serve and worship a Holy God without fear of rejection.

The rewards for having clean hands and a pure heart are significant: you will receive blessings from the God of your salvation, experience answered prayers and have the privilege of approaching the throne of grace with confidence, where you can obtain mercy and find grace in times of need.

Let us strive to have clean hands, intercessors, so that our prayers are not hindered.

PURE HEART

Having a pure heart encompasses being honest, sincere, and devoted to God. It means having a heart free from sin, unforgiveness, or ill feelings towards anyone—a heart fully surrendered to God. Only God can truly cleanse a person's heart, and His word, when taken into your heart, can assist in this transformative process.

- A clean heart is one void of fear, malice, treachery, guilt, shame, and all forms of evil. It will be evident through your words and your attitude towards others. As the Bible says, 'You shall know them by their fruits' **(Matthew 7:16).**

If you speak and act in ways that are hurtful and mean, it indicates that your heart is not yet pure and in need of purification and healing.

- **Matthew 12:34-35**further emphasizes this truth: 'O generation of vipers, how can you, being evil, say good things? For out of the abundance of the heart the mouth speaks. A good man out of the good treasure of his heart brings forth good things, and an evil man out of the evil treasure brings forth evil things.'

Let us strive for pure hearts, allowing God's word to cleanse and heal us so that our lives may reflect His goodness and love.

As someone called to be an intercessor for God, you carry the great responsibility of seeking healing and deliverance from anything in your heart that could hinder you from entering the Father's presence. This book is not meant to bring judgment on anyone, but rather to provide direction and clarity based on God's Word, helping you to fulfill your role as an intercessor with power and effectiveness.

We must do it God's way! The Word says, 'All have sinned and fall short of the glory of God' **(Romans 3:23)**. None of us can judge others. We all need to heal and correct aspects of ourselves before we are ready and qualified to move to the next level.

Let us grow and ascend together, remembering that only those with a pure heart will see God **(Matthew 5:8)**.

Chapter 3

Soul Lifted Up To Idoles

What are Idols and What is Considered Idolatry?

An idol is an object of extreme devotion, which can be an image or statue regarded as equal to or greater than God. Idols can be made from materials such as wood or stone, but idolatry is not limited to physical objects. People can be idols and idolized in the hearts of many, placing them in a position that belongs only to God.

Idolatry involves attributing divine qualities to what is not God. A person commits idolatry whenever they honor or revere a creature or creation in place of God. This could include gods or demons, as seen in practices like Satanism.

God hates idolatry because it falsely represents His nature and character, making statements about Him that are untrue. Idolatry distorts the image of God, reducing Him to something made in the image of man, thereby diminishing His divine majesty and all that makes Him God Almighty. Idolatry can take many forms, but at its core, it always misrepresents the true nature of God.

EXAMPLES OF IDOLS

OBSESSION TO THESE THINGS NOT THE THING ITSELF

- Money
- Fame
- Power
- Social media popularity
- Wealth
- Some relationships
- Material possession
- Excessive attachment to political candidates
- Sports team obsession.
- Celebrities
- People in general
- Mega Church leaders and small churches

SWEARING DECEITFULLY

To swear means to make a solemn statement or promise, affirming that something is true or committing to do something. As an intercessor, being a person of integrity is crucial. One of the qualifications is honesty —being truthful and not swearing falsely, even if it causes you pain or requires personal sacrifice. When you make a promise, you have a responsibility to keep your word, maintaining the integrity of your good name and the anointing on your life. The Word of God says, 'A good name is to be chosen rather than great riches.' If your word cannot be trusted or respected, you have nothing. People grant favor to those who honor their word. They are revered as individuals of integrity.

A notable example of this is someone with an excellent credit history. When a person consistently repays their debts, the credit bureaus report this behavior on your credit report, making companies more willing to extend credit because they trust that person's commitment to repay. Similarly, a good credit history shows that you are someone who keeps their promises. When I worked diligently to improve my credit score, I reached a level where, when purchasing a new vehicle, I could do so with just my signature and no money down. This was because my credit history demonstrated that I honor my word to repay. In God's kingdom, it is the same. He expects you to be the person of your word, no matter the circumstances. Sometimes this requires sacrifice—going without certain things to fulfill your commitments. Being chosen by God to intercede for others is a sacred duty that demands integrity and honesty.

If you want to be an intercessor whose prayers God hears, you must align your life with what He requires, not just what you think is right. We cannot expect God to accept our finite ideas of what is acceptable. God commands us all to pray, but scripture indicates there are prerequisites. Keep praying, even if you do not have everything together immediately. God, in His loving mercy and kindness, may still hear our prayers, especially in times of emergency. God does what He wants, when He wants, and does not need our approval or permission to perform His will.

God's point is clear: Do not make it a habit to enter His presence with dirty hands and a dirty heart.

THE MAKING OF A TRUE INTERCESSOR

Long before you can access God's throne as an active employee of heaven, God takes you through rigorous training to prove you. What does training look like for an intercessor?

- **Recognizing a calling:**Understanding and acknowledging your divine calling.
- **Accepting that call**: Embracing your role with commitment and dedication.
- **Called to a season of preparation**: Undergoing a period where you refine and strengthen your spiritual capacities.
- **Allocating alone time (not loneliness)**: Especially challenging for those married with kids, this involves learning how to balance family and God. You will need to manage your time effectively to pray and study the word. A helpful prayer might be, "Lord, help me number my days and manage my time wisely with all you have given me: family, work, and responsibilities."
- **Feeling Godly burdens for people or situations**: Developing a deep, empathetic concern for others and the issues they face.
- **Always wanting to help people in need**: A natural desire to assist and support those who are struggling.
- **Challenged to deposit the entire written word of God into your spirit**: This involves reading and listening to His word, encompassing both the New and Old Testament, until you fully internalize it.
- **Fasting as instructed by the Holy Spirit**: If you are on medication, continue taking it. Only fast if you are physically able to, and consider alternatives like fasting from TV, social media, or fast food if you cannot fast from food for health reasons.

- **Quickly asking for forgiveness when you make mistakes**: Acknowledge slip-ups and learn from them without excessive self-reproach.
- **Forgiving all**: Essential for maintaining a pure heart. Be vigilant as the enemy will try to create offensive scenarios through close contacts. Recognize that Satan's tricks are common and should not take you by surprise. Offenses will inevitably occur, so forgive quickly and release any grudges. Remember, we do not battle against flesh and blood; personal offenses are merely distractions meant to derail your spiritual mission. Stay focused on your divine assignment.

This structured approach not only outlines the necessary steps but also emphasizes the spiritual and practical disciplines required to be an effective intercessor.

A Burden to Pray

Intercessors will have a burden to pray. Burden: defined as something that is carried, a responsibility or duty, or the carrying of heavy loads. The Holy Spirit often burdens a person to pray His will on Earth. This burden could be for salvation, healing, deliverance, and miracles.

The effectual fervent prayers of a righteous man avail much. **(James 5:16)**

God's Love in Your Heart Is a Prerequisite

Having the agape love of God deep in your heart is mandatory for being a God-ordained intercessor. **Romans 5:5** tells us, "Because the love of God is shed abroad in our hearts by the Holy Spirit, which is given to us."

- **1 Thessalonians 4:9:**Emphasizes brotherly love: "But as touching brotherly love, you need not that I write unto you: for you yourselves are taught of God to love one another."
- **1 Corinthians 13:1-2:**Speaks powerfully about the necessity of love in spiritual gifts:

"If I speak in the tongues of men and of angels, but have not love, I am a noisy gong or a clanging cymbal. And if I have prophetic powers, and understand all mysteries and all knowledge, and if I have all faith, so as to move mountains, but have no love, I am nothing."

It is by the love of God we are compelled to pray or to intercede for people, places, and situations. It is not by our own desires but by the desire of God. He places His desires in our hearts to pray because He loves us so much. The Bible tells us that the Lord sits at the right hand of the Father making intercession for us (Romans 8:34).

Chapter 4

The 5-Fold Ministry Honor

I am deeply grateful for the entire gifts to the body of Christ. In my book, I would like to honor those of any 5-fold ministry office. If you stand legally in one of these offices, I salute you and respect you all for what you do. Being part of the 5-fold ministry is not an easy task. I recognize the challenging work and sacrifices you all make, and it does not go unnoticed.

I want every one of you reading this book to know you are valued more than you know. Your labor shall not be in vain. Though you have experienced much heartache, betrayal, disloyalty, and disappointment from those you served, God wants you to know great is your reward. You have not taken revenge nor given up, even when faced with actions done behind your back by people you trusted who did not appreciate what you have done for them personally. You gave money, cars, paid rent, bought groceries, and prayed for them out of some bad situations and relationships.

Do not feel discouraged or dismayed for your heavenly Father witnessed it all. For your shame, you shall receive double blessings for everything you have given over the years. Continue to be steadfast and unmovable, always abounding in the word of truth. Your God has your back! Receive new strength, life, and a breath of fresh air. Your work is not in vain nor are you finished, even if you must make some minor adjustments. Stay encouraged, for the Lord your God is with you!

TALKING TO GOD IS A PRIVILEGE

God is the awesome and amazing deity that created all things. It is only by His grace that we can even speak with Him. He is all-powerful, all-knowing, and present everywhere at the same time. The ultimate being who is sovereign and holy, He created everything in heaven and on earth. He is the first and the last, the Alpha and Omega, the beginning, and the end. The one and only true living God, He has the power to destroy both body and soul in hell. He is **'INCREATED'**—existing eternally, without ever being created by anyone or anything. He is full of love and mercy for all humankind, having sent His only begotten Son to die for our sins. The Almighty God!

Through the shedding of the blood of His Son, we are now able to commune with Him because the blood of Christ covers our sins. We should be grateful that He gives us access to Him and all of who He is. It is an absolute privilege and honor to have such an amazing invitation to stand before a great King! Do not take this for granted.

I believe that as believers, we have become so familiar and accustomed to being able to talk to God that we lose sight of His greatness and the importance of who He is. My prayer is that every intercessor receives a true revelation of who God our Father is and reverences Him as such. Though God allows us to freely come to Him, we must not lose the respect, honor, and understanding that we are speaking to the highest being ever—the God of all things, who stands alone in His greatness as a mighty King!

He is the most holy, the most supreme, the most sovereign, the most excellent, the only one who is perfect and good. Let us always remember who we are praying to: **He is the Highest.**

He Is Greater Than Any President or Any Higher Office or Priesthood [Respectfully Saying]

Just think about how much respect and honor it is to be able to meet the president of your country. If anyone from the White House or your country's government invites you to meet your president, you would become so nervous and excited to the point of not knowing what to say. If you ever visit the White House and meet the President, who is a person just like you, there are many security protocols you will have to endure beforehand. You would pay close attention to your appearance, your clothing, hair and how you smell. You would not stand before the president in just any manner. You would enter his presence with a sense of respect and reverence because of who he is.

If you would do this for someone who has blood running through their veins just like you, who is a mere creature whom God created, why don't we understand that we should offer God that type of reverence and respect when we try to enter His presence? He is the creator of all, including your president. God expects that we come to Him neatly groomed in the spirit, smelling good, clean, and pure from fleshly sins. The bottom line is that we cannot come before the Father in just any kind of way.

Now I understand the scripture that says man looks at the outward appearance, while God looks at a man's heart. It is not what a man eats that destroys him but what comes out of his mouth, and what comes out of his mouth comes directly from his heart. If your heart is wicked, your words will be also. With a defiled heart, you will begin to pray prayers born from your wickedness and flesh, and not from a place of purity and righteousness. This is why you can hear people praying death and cursing with a judgmental spirit, on people who have wronged them. If you pray with a judgmental tongue, you are not ready. God says, "Bless and curse not." How can you pray prayers that are contrary to His word?

This is why it is mandatory to know God's word in its entirety before you become a kingdom intercessor. This is why it is mandatory to get healed and delivered before God chooses you to be one of His intercessors. Many are called, but few are chosen because only a few are willing to pay the price to allow God to prepare them and are willing to submit to the cleansing process. Others are not willing.

Chapter 5

Pray With Knowledge And Understanding

If the Holy Spirit instructs you to pray for missing, kidnapped, or trafficked children, the first thing you should do is gather information and research the topic thoroughly. Start by reading and learning about child trafficking: find out which areas have the highest reports of this crime and understand the tactics and networks used by traffickers. The more information you have, the better you can form a solid, focused prayer.

Use the information you gather to pray specifically for what is to stop, block, dismantle, and expose these criminal operations. Ask the Holy Spirit to guide you on how to pray effectively for this cause. You may also feel a burden to pray for the families of the missing children, who are suffering deeply due to their child's absence.

Always invite the Holy Spirit into your prayer session. He will guide you and provide you with the right words and focus, revealing things that may not be apparent from your research. The Holy Spirit knows the heart of God and will help you align your prayers with God's will, ensuring that your intercession is both powerful and effective.

FAITH IS THE SUBSTANCE OF THINGS HOPED FOR BUT THE EVIDENCE OF THINGS NOT SEEN [Hebrews 11:1]

It is **impossible** to be an intercessor or a prayer warrior without faith. If you lack faith, you might as well go home, because nothing is going to happen for you. As the younger generation so eloquently puts it, period. Part of your training to become a true intercessor is the development of your faith. Jesus said, "If you have faith as small as a mustard seed, you can say to this mountain, 'Move from here to there,' and it will move. Nothing will be impossible for you" **(Matthew 17:20)**. Wow! This is why it is so important to let God have His way in your life—He knows exactly what to allow in your life to assist with your faith development.

I remember in my earlier years, when I was first introduced to prayer and fasting, I had a situation in my family involving my oldest niece and first-born granddaughter, Anetria Brackett, whom we all lovingly called Ne-Ne. Ne-Ne was graduating from high school as the valedictorian of her class, she was beautiful and smart. Anetria was like a daughter to me, she loved me, and I loved her so very much. I am still grieving the recent loss of this precious soul.

To make a long story short, Anetria's high school only gave each graduate four tickets to give to proud family members. Unfortunately, because Anetria's mom, dad, and grandparents had priority, I and others who wanted to go felt left out without tickets and had to sadly miss the graduation. But being who I am, I was not willing to just sit this one out.

I wanted Ne-Ne to know her auntie was proud of her, supported her, and celebrated all her accomplishments. I wanted her to see my face, even if it was just in the parking lot of her high school.

As I drove to the graduation site, I was determined to get in, even without a ticket. I started thinking of different elaborate lies I could tell to convince someone to let me in. But as I pulled up to the high school with my son in the back seat, I heard in my spirit, "If you try to think of lies to tell someone, you are literally consulting with the prince of lies, who is the devil. When you yield yourself to lies, you are asking Satan for help."

I paused and asked God to forgive me. I had no idea that I was doing that, and I did not realize that God was teaching me how to live by faith. In that same moment, I repented, and the Lord moved upon my heart to simply ask if I could come in and to tell the truth. He instructed me to be honest, and I thought, "Okay, let's do it."

My son and I walked to the entrance of the school, where other proud family and friends were eagerly waiting to get inside. When I finally got to the door, I saw a tall, bald security guard standing next to a sweet-looking lady who seemed like a teacher. I walked up to the table where they were collecting tickets and, remembering what the Lord had told me, I said, "Excuse me, ma'am, my niece is graduating today, and I do not have a ticket, but I would really like to see her graduate."

The lady looked at me for about half a second, then beckoned me with her hand to come in. I was absolutely amazed at how the outcome turned in my favor through a simple act of obedience. Not only did she let me into the graduation, but she also allowed my son to come in with me. That day marked the beginning of my faith walk with God. He reminded me to always follow that voice I heard that day.

I learned that my faith not only opens doors for me but also for my family and others. The Word of God says, "The just shall live by faith," and that it is impossible to please God without faith. True intercessors must have faith to believe God for things on behalf of their families and others. **Faith is an intercessor's universal key!** Not just for intercessors, but for every believer.

So, as you prepare for your journey, do not be surprised if you find yourself in situations that challenge you to exercise your faith. There are people waiting for your development who need your help. Will you allow the Holy Spirit to do His work inside you? You are necessary to the kingdom of God.

Chapter 6

Are You In His Presence Or On The Battlefied

This book, written to clarify a common misunderstanding among many who do not grasp the difference between communing with God versus being in a spiritual battle actively waging war against the enemy. Let me set the stage for a moment—crack my knuckles, roll up my sleeves, and take a sip of water before diving into this discussion. Over my years in various corporate prayer settings, I have observed both commendable and less desirable practices. I urge everyone to come closer and pay keen attention to what I am about to share; this revelation will provide you with much-needed understanding and insight.

In our prayer lives, whether corporately or privately, some believers are led to believe that engaging in spiritual warfare—binding and loosing, tearing down the kingdom of darkness, blocking fiery darts in the spiritual realm, and declaring that the gates of hell shall not prevail—is synonymous with praying or communing with God. This is not the case. Engaging in warfare is crucial work; do not stop or come down from it. However, it is important to recognize that engaging in warfare is different from praying or communing with God. These are two distinctly different experiences.

While engaged in war, we are on a spiritual battleground, not in an intimate communing atmosphere with God, which we call the prayer of intercession. Many of God's children mistakenly believe that after battling the enemy in the spirit, they have been in prayer. This is incorrect. Prayer with God involves direct communication where we talk to Him, and He talks to us. It is where we let our requests be known to Him, where we ask Him to bless and help people—not fight.

Imagine a war zone with opposing sides fighting, using bombs, assault weapons, and chemicals—can you have an intimate time and fellowship with anyone under such circumstances? The answer is a resounding no. Spending time with God means talking to Him and listening as He speaks, not engaging in combat. Fighting should be for a time separate from communing with God.

If you find yourself always battling and never sitting quietly at His feet, you are missing the essence of what it means to be in God's presence. We should be fostering a quality relationship with Him, sitting quietly before Him, or interceding for others, rather than constantly fighting. By failing to distinguish these two, many fall under the deception of the enemy.

Remember the words of God in **Matthew 7:22-23:** "Many will say to me on that day, 'Lord, Lord, did we not prophesy in your name and in your name drive out demons and, in your name, perform many miracles?' Then I will tell them plainly, 'I never knew you. Away from me, you evildoers!'" You may do great work, but if you forget to take off your war garments, clean up, and come sit with the Father in prayer, you miss out on the intimacy He desires.

Afterwards, you can put your war clothes back on, return to battle, and continue your spiritual warfare. God wants to fellowship with you, to instruct and impart wisdom into you before you go into battle. Understand the difference. Do not confuse warfare intercession with communing or talking to God!

DON'T USE YOUR POWER FOR EVIL

This is why God takes us intercessors through a rigorous training process. You must have your emotions in check. Uncontrolled emotions can get you into trouble and cause you to sin with your mouth and gifts by speaking and praying negative things against someone who has angered you. The Word of God says to love your enemies, bless those who curse you, do good to those who hate you, and pray for those who spitefully use you and persecute you **(Matthew 5:44)**. We must trust God and His word, understanding that every word He speaks is with a divine purpose and reason.

If we curse people with our mouths, we end up cursing ourselves, because we reap what we sow. If you sow love, you will receive love. If you sow hate, hate will return to you. This is why the Lord told Peter, who cut off the ear of one of the men who came to arrest Jesus, "If you live by the sword, you shall perish by it" **(Matthew 26:52)**. Because of the spiritual law that says, "You shall reap what you sow," which some call "karma."

So, to my fellow intercessors, be careful what you say to others and in prayer. Heaven is listening. Remember, long before God trusts you with real power, He will test you by giving you a little power to see if your ability to control what comes out of your mouth. The power of life and death begins with the tongue, but God encourages us to speak life! I believe that authorization to speak of death should be for those who are mature, seasoned, and understand how to flow in the power of God without being destructive and messy.

Too many of God's people are found guilty of speaking curses over one another; that is why your power is limited. If you want God to remove the limitations of your gift, grow up and be more responsible with it. God is wise and extremely intelligent. If your power matched your knowledge, most of the world and the people in it would destroy themselves because of spiritual immaturity.

I am so grateful for God's loving mercy and grace on all of humanity. There is one instance in the Word where the Lord cursed the fig tree for being fruitless **(Mark 11:12-25)**. When it comes to people the Word of God tells us to bless and curse not. (Romans 12:14) Curses are from a place of anger, even hate. If curses come out of your mouth towards a person, this speaks volumes about the condition of your heart. Bitter and sweet water cannot come from the same fountain.

Prayer Burdens

- Prophetic intercessory prayer
- Government
- Community
- Political
- Marketplace
- Education
- Family and marriage
- Lost souls, including backsliders.
- Agriculture and our food
- Healing and deliverance
- The body of Christ
- Israel and Jerusalem
- Our military
- Media and entertainment
- At-risk boys and girls
- Human trafficking
- All illegal activities

These areas highlight the diverse burdens that intercessors may carry, calling for focused prayer and spiritual intervention to bring about God's will on Earth.

Chapter 7

What Is Prophetic Intercession

Having the ability to hear and see in the realm of the spirit concerning things God would have you pray about is, to put it plainly, praying the will of God based on what He shows you in prayer.

This is one of my favorites. Prophetic intercession is one of the best forms of prayer because it removes the guesswork from what to pray. When you understand that you are merely a finite being who knows little about the hidden aspects of people, places, and things, you realize that you can only rely on the Spirit of God, who is omnipresent, all-knowing, and all-powerful. He will reveal to you that for which you ought to pray.

Yes, we can look at the news to see what is happening or pay attention to the events occurring in our family and community. However, we come to know that things in the natural world cannot be compared to what the Lord can show you in the spiritual realm. The natural realm can report a mass shooting that has taken place in a particular city or state with unfortunate loss of life, but prophetic sight in prayer can see it before it happens and pray against it. You can save many live and the only thing required is your obedience in prayer.

Over the years, I have heard people of faith pronounce destruction over people and even our country. They claim that God showed them things to come as a warning. I believe these warnings may have some validity. Nevertheless, as prophetic people, when God shows us warnings —whether through your own vision or visions others have seen—it is our job as prophetic intercessors to take those warnings to God and seek direction on what to do next.

There have been many times when I have heard warnings given, even "false" prophecies proclaimed, that the Lord instructed me to "block" in the spirit and forbid it to happen. You can prevent these things from manifesting through the power of His word. I want to teach you how to block attacks from the enemy and how to prophetically stop what the enemy wants to do in your life, family, city, or state. It is all done through the power of God's word and the power of your tongue, by faith.

We as believers must stop accepting everything the enemy says or threatens to do through people, regardless of who they are. All Satan needs is agreement from people who have heard the demonic declaration that he placed in the hearts of certain individuals to speak out of their mouths. Do not be deceived because they wear titles and stand in certain offices, often appointed by themselves. If what that person is speaking does not line up with the word of God, it is a "lie." Be on guard and be wise.

Remember—and I am repeating this so you can etch it in your heart —every time the devil uses someone to speak words of death and destruction over a person, people, places, or things, **he is looking for agreement from you so that he can manifest his will and diabolical plan.** He understands the power of agreement very well. He also knows that nothing can move unless he plants the seed through a spoken word first. Then, he knows he needs to water that seed with the power of your agreement and needs as many people as he can get to start speaking his demonic vision. Just like that, HIS will is accomplished.

Once His will has been fulfilled, people often say things like, "See, that person must truly be from God; they spoke it, and now see what happened. Bishop Joe Blow died a horrible death just as they spoke." God said, "Speak life and not death," and He said, "Bless and curse not." So, if anyone does these things, they are speaking contrary to the word. As prophetic intercessors, our job is not to judge matters but to pray according to the will of the Father.

SILENCE IN PRAYER

"Keep your foot when you go into the house of God; be more ready to hear than to give the sacrifice of fools, for they do not consider that they are doing evil. Be not rash with your mouth and let not your heart be hasty to utter anything before God. God is in heaven, and you are on earth; therefore, let your words be few."

How many times have we entered prayer with God and prayed for a whole hour, only to immediately walk away to go about our day, never being mindful that God may want to speak? Do you ever just go into your prayer room silently? As much as God loves to hear your voice, He also wants you to come before Him sometimes with a quiet spirit. Praying is not only about petitioning God for things but also about receiving instruction and insight. Being quiet before the Lord allows you the opportunity to hear God's voice just as much as He hears yours.

Sometimes we think we have everything all figured out when we talk to God. We may even try to tell Him what He should do instead of allowing Him to impart divine wisdom to us. Being quiet in prayer takes discipline. Before I begin to speak to our Holy Father, I always ask Him to forgive me of all my sins first—the sins I know about and the ones I do not know about. I might have some soft worship songs playing extremely low, just to prepare the atmosphere for communing with God.

Some people may light candles—I do not, but whatever God leads you to do is fine.

I have found that when you are quiet during your prayer session, God can minister to you. There have been times when I would just begin to weep or feel the burden of praying for certain people or situations. One thing that is for sure, without a shadow of a doubt, is that when you are before the Lord in prayer and are truly seeking Him and His perfect will for yourself, the first thing God will minister to you about will be connected to what's in your heart that is offensive to people. How do I know this? In a very intense encounter with God in prayer one day, I heard Him say I was mean. I began to see the faces of people I was being mean to. He challenged me to fix that aspect of my character.

Before God reveals anything to you about anyone else, He's going to show you what is wrong with you first. As Matthew 7:5 says, "First cast the beam out of your own eye, then you will be able to see clearly to cast out the mote out of your brother's eye."

James 1:19 says, "Let every man be swift to hear but slow to speak."

A wise person will recognize that when you come before a great and mighty King, you should be silent to receive His wisdom, knowing that you are talking to someone greater and wiser than you. We should use every precious moment we spend in prayer to seek to hear what He has to say.

One powerful thing I found out years ago, and this revelation is what prompts me to be more attentive and eager to know God's written word. I will share with you what I learned:

Long before you hear God's audible voice, you must hear His voice through His written word.

What does this mean? The written word of God is His voice. If you cannot obey that voice first, you will not be able to hear Him when He speaks audibly. To hear is to obey Him. This is a message to all my intercessors: **If you want to be able to hear God, learn His word thoroughly, and obey what you have learned. Then He will utter things to you that others desire to know and hear but cannot.**

> Matthew 13:17 says, "Many have desired to see the things which you see and have not seen, and to hear the things you hear and have not."

God often speaks in a still, small voice because He desires a relationship with us that is based on faith, trust, and obedience. If we are not willing or able to listen to and obey His written Word, which He has already provided for guidance and instruction, we may not be ready to hear His more direct, audible voice. God is wise and does things with purpose and order. How faithfully we respond to His written Word demonstrates our readiness to hear and follow His audible guidance. This progression reflects a deeper level of spiritual maturity and a closer relationship with God.

Chapter 8

The Secret Place

What You Do in Secret, God Will Reward Openly (Matthew 6:4)

The intercessor's greatest place for effectiveness is in the secret place of their prayer closet. Yes, corporate prayer is great and appreciated, but there is nothing like that secret place in prayer. I have seen more prayers answered in my secret place than anywhere else, especially as I pray for others. It is in your secret place of prayer that God will show you who and for what to pray. There are some things I have had the burdened to pray for that I cannot mention in this book. True intercessors are God's secret weapons on earth.

Everything God shows you is not meant for social media; broadcasting these revelations can compromise your spiritual covering. It is vital to understand your ranking in the spirit realm. Knowing your ranking and level of authority will determine how you pray and see spiritually. Just like in real life, the higher you rise, the more you can see. Can God trust you enough to share things with you that you will not go and tell others?

There are things that God will show His intercessors that He does not want publicized on social media platforms or even shared with another person—things that are of a sensitive nature. Let me share a true story that illustrates this. I knew my spiritual ranking had shifted when I saw this. One day in April 2021, I was looking out of my living room window, casually watching what was happening outside my home, when I saw a quick glimpse of actor Bill Cosby in my mind's eye. Along with his image, I saw the word "RELEASED" in big, bold letters.

I remember thinking to myself, "Is Bill Cosby released from jail?" I quickly grabbed my cell phone to do a Google search to see if he was out of jail because I had not followed the story closely after his arrest. I sat on my living room sofa, googling Bill Cosby, and discovered that he was still in jail with a sentence of up to 10 years. At that point, I was unclear why I had this vision. I put my phone down, and the next thing I heard was, "Pray for Bill Cosby and open the prison door for him; I am sending him home."

I will do my best to describe what happened next. When I stood up, I felt as if a court-appointed authority had come down from heaven, put a court-authorized document in my hand, and told me to execute this order. It felt so real! The order was "RELEASE BILL COSBY FROM PRISON." It was so strong on me that I could not help but obey. I proceeded to pray with clear, precise words: "I declare and decree that Bill Cosby shall not die in jail. I command an immediate RELEASE OF HIM NOW," just as I had seen it.

I know this sounds bizarre and unbelievable to some, but it happened just as I spoke it. Not even two months later, I was sitting in that same living room watching the local news when a special report popped up "Actor Bill Cosby - Released from Prison." I jumped up and yelled down to the lower level of our home where my husband was working, "They let Bill Cosby out of jail!" I screamed with excitement. I was so glad I had told someone, particularly my husband, when I first received the vision and assignment to pray for him, so people would not think I was making this story up. I have nothing to prove or gain by doing so.

My purpose in sharing this is purely educational. My husband ran up the stairs, wondering if I was okay because of my excitement. Once he found out I was fine and why I was excited, he jokingly asked, "Do you think you can get R. Kelly out of jail?" I said jokingly, "Sir, please go have a seat."

I also told him it does not work like that. That is when I received the revelation that when something like this happens, there must be an order from heaven and not just something you do because you want to pray someone out of prison. There are spiritual protocols that must be adhered to.

This had nothing to do with me or what I personally wanted to see happen. I did not follow Mr. Cosby like that. This came to me in a vision, and then I simply prayed about what I saw. I realized in that moment the importance of obeying God. When you pray for His will, things move. I also realized at that moment that someone from Bill Cosby's circle must have gotten a prayer through that God answered and approved. I learned that no matter what people may think should happen to us because of what wrong they believe we have done, God has the final say.

Mr. Cosby was also in prison praying and even asked for forgiveness of his sins, if any—who knows? All I know is God said to pray him out. I am sure many people were not happy with that outcome; nevertheless, God is in control. I discovered that the reason for his release was because his due process rights had been violated.

I am telling you, there is something powerful about secret place intercession. If someone reading this knows Bill Cosby or anyone close to him, tell him I said, "You're welcome." I am so kidding, God gets all the glory; He was the one who sent His anointing to free him, not me. God

used my mouth—that is it. God did it! And no, I cannot release your
Uncle Bobby out of jail; God did not send me the paperwork for him, lol.

Chapter 9

Can God Trust You?

Long before God trusts you with deep secrets, He will evaluate you to see how well you can "hold water." What do I mean? As an intercessor, you will quickly learn that before God allows you to access deep realms of revelation, He will show you things and challenge you to maintain silence, then watch to see if you will obey. Obedience is better than sacrifice (1 Samuel 15:22). Part of being an intercessor is knowing what to say and what not to say, what to share openly, and what to keep in your prayer closet.

It can be exciting when we are shown things in the spirit, and by nature, we may want to tell the world what we see. However, discretion is required when it comes to certain things the Lord will have you pray for. For example, if the Lord shows you an attempt on the president's life or someone with a high profile, whether political or of celebrity status, you cannot go around telling everyone or posting on social media what you see. You may end up with the Secret Service knocking at your door, wondering how you know and if you have something to do with it. So, be wise. If the Lord shows you things like that in prayer, just pray for their safety and ask God to expose every plan and plot to harm anyone He shows you.

God Trusts the Judgment of His Righteous Intercessors

When you have dedicated your life to intercessory prayer and God has proven you through many tests and trials, and you have been found with clean hands and a heart free of judgment, and you are deeply connected with the Holy Spirit and led by His Spirit, God can trust your judgment in matters when it comes to pleading someone's cause in prayer.

Will God give a man the ability to decide? Yes! In the book of **Genesis 2:19**, "Out of the ground the Lord God formed every beast of the field, and every fowl of the air, and brought them to Adam to see what he would name them. And whatever Adam called each living creature, that was its name." Adam was given the authority to name all the animals God had created. God trusted Adam to operate in his authority because he was connected to God. This was a true testament to Adam's relationship with the Creator.

Remember, this was a time and place before the fall of man through disobedience. So, it is safe to say that sin can cause you to lose or abort your authority, but obedience can cause you to walk in great power and grace. As intercessors, we must be also connected to God that He can trust us as His righteous sons and daughters to make the right decisions in prayer because we have a complete and unwavering understanding of His character, ways, likes, and dislikes. Can God trust you like that? **Psalm 25:14** "The secret of the Lord is with those who fear Him, and He will show them His covenant."

Chapter 10

What Is A Secret

A secret is something that is not known or not meant to be known or seen by others. God confides in certain people—those who fear Him. God will share His deepest, most intimate secrets with those who dedicate themselves to Him in prayer in the secret place. The more time you spend with the Father, the closer you get to Him, the more of His heart He will reveal to you. To know the secrets of God, we must draw close to Him.

Hebrews 11:6 says, "Without faith, it is impossible to please Him: for he who comes to God must believe that He is, and that He is a rewarder of those who diligently seek Him."

Types of Intercessors

1. **Warfare Intercessors**: These intercessors are engaged in high-level spiritual warfare. They focus on binding and losing and are familiar with demonic hierarchies, principalities, powers, and rulers in dark places.

2. **Transformational Intercessors**: These intercessors pray prophetically for what is needed for a city, church, business, state, country, or global affairs. They stand in the gap, asking for forgiveness and mercy, and pray against the works of the enemy.

3. **Political Intercessors**: These intercessors are burdened to pray for matters in the political realm, covering all branches of government. They do not impose their opinions but pray for God's will to be done rather than the will of people.

4. **Crisis Intercessors**: Crisis intercessors pray for emergency situations such as natural disasters, pandemics, epidemics, mass shootings, human trafficking, and illegal drug transportation. They understand how to anticipate and block potential crises in the spirit realm.

5. **Birthing and Midwife Intercessors**: These intercessors know how to pray things into manifestation in the spirit. They are used to bring souls into the kingdom of God and pray to usher in God's will for families, communities, cities, and individuals.

6. **Personal Intercessors**: Personal intercessors focus on praying for individuals, children, marriages, families, pastors, and friends. They pray for immediate needs, desires, healing, deliverance, guidance, forgiveness of sins, and salvation.

7. **Marketplace Intercessors**: These intercessors cover businesses, technology, the stock market, banking systems, the real estate market, economic structures, fairness, and healthcare.

8. **Missions Intercessors**: Missions intercessors pray for missionaries worldwide, focusing on protection and provision for those on the mission field.

9. **Regional Intercessors**: These intercessors pray against regional demonic spirits. They understand the spiritual dynamics and entities operating in the specific regions they live in.

Chapter 11

How Should I Pray?

Matthew 6:5-13 Provides Guidance on Prayer:

- **Verses 5-6**: "When you pray, don't be like the hypocrites who love to pray standing in the synagogues and on the street corners to be seen by others. Truly I tell you, they have received their reward in full. But when you pray, go into your room, close the door, and pray to your Father, who is unseen. Then your Father, who sees what is done in secret, will reward you."
- **Verses 7-8**: "And when you pray, do not keep on babbling like pagans, for they think they will be heard because of their many words. Do not be like them, for your Father knows what you need before you ask Him."
- **Verses 9-13**: Jesus provides a model prayer, commonly known as the Lord's Prayer, emphasizing acknowledging God, seeking His will, asking for provision, forgiveness, guidance, and deliverance.

Matthew 26:40 also mentions prayer: "He came to his disciples and found them asleep. He said to Peter, 'Could you not watch with me for one hour?'"

The Bible does not provide a specific time for prayer, but it offers examples. Jesus prayed for an hour in some instances, while other scriptures suggest that long, repetitive prayers are unnecessary.

The Lord's Prayer Model (Matthew 6: 9- 13)

1. **Acknowledgment**: Recognizing who God the Father is ("Our Father").
2. **Praise**: Honoring God's name ("Hallowed be thy name").
3. **God's Will**: Praying for God's kingdom and will to be established on earth as it is in heaven ("Thy kingdom come, thy will be done on earth as it is in heaven").
4. **Provision**: Asking for daily needs ("Give us this day our daily bread").
5. **Forgiveness**: Requesting forgiveness for our sins and forgiving others ("Forgive us our debts, as we forgive our debtors").
6. **Guidance and Protection**: Asking God to lead us away from temptation and deliver us from evil ("Lead us not into temptation but deliver us from evil").
7. **Acknowledgment of God's Sovereignty**: Recognizing God's rule, power, and glory ("For thine is the kingdom, and the power, and the glory, forever, Amen").

Chapter 12

How Long Should I Pray?

The duration of prayer depends on the intercessor. There is not a set formula or time; what matters is following the biblical format while tailoring it to your specific assignment and personal needs in prayer. When praying, be specific, precise, and genuine. Speak to God as if He is in the room with you. You do not need to shout or use a loud voice; God hears even when you speak softly but with confidence. The tone of your prayer may vary depending on whether you are communing with God or engaging in spiritual warfare.

Time Management for Intercessors

Managing your time effectively is crucial for intercessors, especially if you have a busy life with work, family, and other responsibilities. Discipline is key to setting aside dedicated time to commune with God. **Psalm 90:12** says, "So teach us to number our days, that we may apply our hearts unto wisdom." If you are called to be an intercessor, having order in your life is mandatory.

Though it is challenging when you have a lot on your plate, it is possible with strategic planning. For example, you might start your prayer time early in the morning, around 4-5 am, when everyone else is still asleep, or at night when the household is quiet. Choose what works best for your life and make it a consistent practice.

The key is to remain disciplined, intentional, and mindful of the importance of spending time with God. He wants to use you in a great and mighty way, but proper training and preparation are essential. By aligning your life with God's will and managing your time wisely, you can effectively serve as an intercessor, praying for people, places, and situations as the Lord leads you.

Respect My Prayer Time

This is a topic I have discussed with many other intercessors: teaching children and all family members to respect prayer time. Everyone who lives within the four walls of your home should understand that you are a prayer warrior and that you must occasionally leave family engagements to spend time with the Lord. This should not come as a surprise to your household members. There should be consistency in when you choose to pray.

I have learned that family life and work can be so demanding that they can easily cause you to lose focus on your spiritual assignment as an intercessor. Sit your family down and communicate to them exactly who you are and what you must do; this will bring understanding and respect for your prayer time. Clearly explain to your family and friends that when you enter your prayer time with God, that there must not be any interruptions except for emergencies.

During this time of communication with your family, you can create some rules for maintaining quiet around the place where you choose to pray so as not to disturb your flow in the spirit. Clear communication with your family will help them respect you and your prayer time with the Lord. Simple communication can go a long way. When your children see you setting time apart to talk to God, it creates an example they can follow.

What great seeds you would be sowing into your family, who are watching your witness as a faithful servant to God in prayer. This is something they will carry into their lives as adults, and this faithful obedience to the call to intercession can potentially continue from generation to generation in your family because of you.

Chapter 13

I Am Healed

I cannot express enough the importance of allowing the Lord to cleanse and heal you before you fully move into your prayer ministry. I want to speak especially to the prophetic intercessors and those who have the gift of discernment. When you are a wounded soul, you tend to project from that place of woundedness, which can mix with what God wants to show you. Your woundedness contaminates your anointing. Be committed to seeking the Lord for your personal healing so He can use you in a great and mighty way.

Keep Yourself Protected

As an intercessor, we have a responsibility to ensure all doors of corruption and sin are not present in our lives. I cannot stress this enough! Open doors can attract demonic forces that will try to expose your sins, bring shame and embarrassment to you, and destroy or weaken your effectiveness. The Bible says the thief (enemy) seeks to kill, steal, and destroy (John 10:10). You must know and understand that the enemy of your soul does not want you interceding at all; he will try anything he can to stop or hinder you if possible.

We are not ignorant concerning the devil's devices (2 Corinthians 2:11). He understands that if you are praying, his works are impeded. He will slither his way into any crack or crevice in your life to shut your prayer ministry down. The Bible says, "Give no place to the devil" (Ephesians 4:27). Protect yourself and close every open door in your life while you have the grace to do so.

Examples of Open Doors

1. Secret Sin
2. Fornication
3. Adultery
4. Dishonest earnings
5. Lying
6. Cheating on taxes
7. Debt
8. Gambling
9. Unforgiveness
10. Substance abuse
11. Gluttony
12. Stealing
13. Gossiping
14. Poor health
15. Procrastination

Chapter 14

Pray For Yourself

Father, I thank you for giving us all the ability to come boldly to your throne of grace so that we may obtain mercy and find grace to help in a time of need. Your word says men ought always to pray and not to faint. You said to put you in remembrance of your Word. I ask that you first forgive me of my sins so that my prayers are not hindered. I ask that you give me a clean heart and renew in me the right spirit. I forgive and release any person who has hurt me in any way; I ask that you bless them. Your word says to love your enemies, bless those that curse you, and pray for those who despitefully use and persecute you, so I do just that.

If I have hurt or offended anyone, I pray you fill their hearts with forgiveness for me. I ask, Father, that you give me eyes to see in the spirit and ears to hear so I can pray what you would have me pray. I ask that you grant me the faith and power required to manifest your promises, not just for me but for others. Thank you for the anointing of the intercessor that you have given me. May I be qualified to stand in the gap and pray always.

I ask, Father, that you bless me and my family and that your angels protect us always. Let no weapon formed against me prosper. Let not the gates of hell prevail against me. Let me have no successful enemies. I command everything the enemy intended for evil in my life to be turned around for my good. I thank you that I have the victory in all things and that the devil is a defeated foe in my life and family. I thank you for supplying all my needs according to your riches in glory.

I thank you for walking and living in your blessings that make me rich and add no sorrow. Thank you. I am the head and not the tail, the lender and not the borrower. I thank you that I live a debt-free life, and I owe no man anything but to love him. I thank you for living in your favor that gives life. I declare and decree LIFE in every area of my life. I thank you that I live in divine healing. I thank you that I am prosperous in good health, even as my soul is prosperous.

I thank you that my name is written in the Lamb's Book of Life and that goodness and mercy follow me all the days of my life, and I shall dwell in the house of the Lord forever! I thank you, Father, that your promises are yes and amen, and I thank you, Father, that you hear me when I pray!

About the Author

Sherita Mitchell is a testament to the transformative power of faith and the journey of discovering one's spiritual calling. Reflecting on her early days as a new believer, she recalls seasoned members of her faith community telling her, "I see an intercessory prayer mantle on you." At the time, these words felt foreign to her, and she silently wondered, "What is an intercessor?" Despite her initial lack of understanding, Sherita's heart was open to learning and growing.

As she embraced her calling, Sherita took intentional steps to deepen her understanding of intercessory prayer. She began attending prayer meetings, not just as a participant but as a student, keenly observing how others prayed for people and situations beyond their immediate circles. Initially, her prayers were centered around her own needs and those of her family. However, as she spent more time in prayer and immersed herself in literature by great authors on intercessory prayer, her perspective began to shift. She started to see her journey not just as her own spiritual growth but as a way of learning how to stand in the gap for others.

Sherita recognizes that her journey into intercessory prayer has been guided by God's hand from the beginning. She humbly acknowledges that her ability to author this book—or any work on prayer—is not of her own making. "I could not author this book, or any book on prayer, without first acknowledging God, who is the author and finisher of my faith. It is HE who gives us wisdom, knowledge, understanding, and the gifts, talents, and abilities to do all things," Sherita says, reflecting on her journey of faith and discovery of her intercessory calling. She attributes all wisdom, knowledge, understanding, and the gifts she possesses to God.

Through her experiences, Sherita has come to understand that being an intercessor is more than just praying for others; it is about having a heart that aligns with God's, being sensitive to His voice, and standing in faith on behalf of those who may not have the strength or words to pray for themselves. Her journey is a reminder that God often calls us to roles we may not initially understand, but through faith, dedication, and a willingness to learn, He equips us to fulfill our purpose.

For permissions or bookings, please contact: asksherita@yahoo.com

www.ingramcontent.com/pod-product-compliance
Lightning Source LLC
Chambersburg PA
CBHW050809160726
48004CB00002B/767